WOULD YOU RATHER?

BOOK FOR KIDS

Ages 6-12

Our team has put a lot of work into creating this book, we would be grateful for sharing your opinion about it.

SCAN FOR MORE
PRODUCTS

??? ???
... BE INVISIBLE
OR
BE ABLE TO FLY?

WOULD YOU RATHER...

??? ???

... BE A DOLPHIN
OR
A UNICORN?

...BE TWENTY YEARS OLDER OR TEN YEARS YOUNGER?

WOULD YOU RATHER...

... LIVE IN THE SKY OR UNDER THE SEA?

...HAVE 6 SISTERS OR 6 BROTHERS?

WOULD YOU RATHER...

...HAVE A PET GUINEA PIG OR A PET CHINCHILLA?

...BE A DANCER OR A SINGER?

WOULD YOU RATHER...

... EAT RAW EGG OR RAW MEAT?

...EAT CHOCOLATE ALL MONTH OR EAT PIZZA ALL MONTH?

WOULD YOU RATHER...

... GO INTO SPACE OR VISIT TITANIC?

...GO BACK IN TIME OR LIVE 100 YEARS IN THE FUTURE?

WOULD YOU RATHER...

... PLAY CHESS OR PING PONG?

...BE FOREVER YOUNG OR READ MINDS?

WOULD YOU RATHER...

... TO GET AN OSCAR OR A NOBEL PRIZE?

... TO BE A SOCCER OR BASKETBALL CHAMPION?

WOULD YOU RATHER...

... TO BE ONE METER TALL OR THREE METERS TALL?

... TO HAVE A CINEMA AT HOME OR A SWIMMING POOL?

WOULD YOU RATHER...

... TO STAR IN A MOVIE WITH YOUR FAVORITE ACTOR OR SING WITH YOUR IDOL ON ONE STAGE?

... TO RIDE A CAMEL OR A MAMMOTH?

WOULD YOU RATHER...

... TO HAVE THREE ARMS OR THREE LEGS?

... HAVE UNLIMITED SWEETS OR UNLIMITED FRIES?

WOULD YOU RATHER...

... HAVE REALLY SMALL HANDS OR REALLY BIG FEET?

... GO ON A ROLLERCOASTER OR GO SKY DIVING?

WOULD YOU RATHER...

... HAVE THREE MONTHS OF VACATION IN WINTER OR A MONTH OF VACATION IN SUMMER?

... PLAY PAINTBALL OR GO TO THE CLIMBING PARK?

WOULD YOU RATHER...

... TO EAT A DEAD SPIDER OR A LIVE FROG?

... SPEND AN HOUR WITH FRIENDLY TIGERS OR BE AN HOUR WITH UNPLEASANT CATS?

WOULD YOU RATHER...

... TO HAVE FOUR EARS OR FOUR EYES?

... SPEND AN HOUR WITH FRIENDLY TIGERS OR BE AN HOUR WITH UNPLEASANT CATS?

WOULD YOU RATHER...

... BE ABLE TO PLAY ANY MUSICAL INSTRUMENT OR KNOW ALL THE LANGUAGES OF THE WORLD?

... TO HAVE A PINOCCHIO NOSE OR TO HAVE ELF EARS?

WOULD YOU RATHER...

... MEET A DINOSAUR OR A WHALE?

... TO GO TO THE MOON OR VISIT ALL THE COUNTRIES OF THE WORLD?

WOULD YOU RATHER...

... NEVER WASH YOUR HAIR OR CUT YOUR NAILS?

... TO FLY A PARAGLIDER OR A HELICOPTER?

WOULD YOU RATHER...

... TO GO TO THE ZOO OR THE WATER PARK?

... TO BE A FLY OR A WASP?

WOULD YOU RATHER...

... LIVE WITHOUT INTERNET FOR A MONTH OR LIVE A YEAR WITHOUT TV?

... TO EAT A RAW POTATO OR A WHOLE LEMON?

WOULD YOU RATHER...

... TO BUILD A TREEHOUSE OR BUILD AN IGLOO?

... DRINK 5 LITERS OF COLA OR EAT 5 KILOS OF JELLY BEANS?

WOULD YOU RATHER...

... LOSE ONE ARM OR LOSE ONE LEG?

... TO BE RICH OR TO BE THE SMARTEST IN THE WORLD?

WOULD YOU RATHER...

...ALWAYS TAKE A COLD SHOWER OR SLEEP AN HOUR LESS THAN YOU NEED?

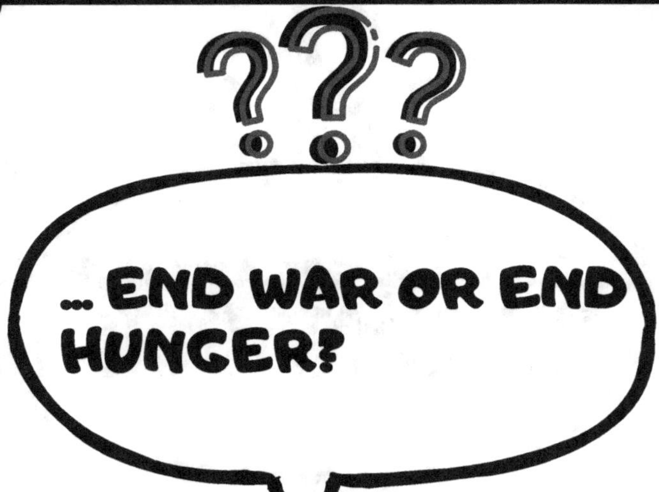

... END WAR OR END HUNGER?
WOULD YOU RATHER...

... MEET A SUPERHERO OR A CARTOON CHARACTER?

... EAT ICE CREAM WITH SALT OR EAT TOMATO WITH SUGAR?

WOULD YOU RATHER...

...HAVE A PIE SMASHED ONTO YOUR FACE OR BE SPRAYED ALL OVER YOUR BODY WITH SILLY STRING?

... HAVE TO BRUSH YOUR TEETH WITH BAKING SODA OR DISH SOAP?

WOULD YOU RATHER...

... LAY IN BED WITH YOUR FAVORITE STUFFED ANIMAL OR YOUR FAVORITE BLANKET?

... HAVE FREE AIRLINE TICKETS FOR LIFE OR A LIFETIME COUPON FOR FREE GROCERY SHOPPING?

WOULD YOU RATHER...

... TO LIVE IN THE COUNTRYSIDE WITH INTERNET ACCESS OR IN A BIG CITY WITHOUT INTERNET?

... TO LIVE BY THE SEA OR IN THE MOUNTAINS?

WOULD YOU RATHER...

... TO HAVE A HIPPO'S NOSE OR AN ELEPHANT'S TRUNK?

... HAVE TEETH THAT GLOW IN THE DARK OR HAIR THAT GLOWS IN THE DARK?

WOULD YOU RATHER...

... LOSE EVERY BOARD GAME YOU PLAY OR BURN EVERYTHING YOU TRY TO COOK?

... HAVE TEETH THAT GLOW IN THE DARK OR HAIR THAT GLOWS IN THE DARK?

WOULD YOU RATHER...

... LOSE EVERY BOARD GAME YOU PLAY OR BURN EVERYTHING YOU TRY TO COOK?

... BE THE OLDEST SIBLING OR THE YOUNGEST SIBLING?

WOULD YOU RATHER...

... HAVE YOUR GRANDMOTHER'S HAIRSTYLE OR FIRST NAME?

... PASS OUT EVERY 5 MINUTES OR POOP 20 TIMES A DAY

WOULD YOU RATHER...

... MAKE LION SOUNDS OR SING LIKE A BIRD?

... WEAR A CLOWN OUTFIT FOR A WEEK OR WEAR GRANDMA'S CLOTHES FOR A WEEK?

WOULD YOU RATHER...

... NOT TO BRUSH YOUR TEETH FOR A MONTH OR NOT TO WASH YOUR HANDS FOR A MONTH?

...HAVE TO USE A PUBLIC TOILET THAT IS EXTREMELY DIRTY AND DARK OR ONE THAT HAS A SNAKE IN IT?

WOULD YOU RATHER...

... EAT DOG FOOD OR EAT AN INEDIBLE MUSHROOM?

... NEVER TO BE ABLE TO EAT YOUR FAVORITE FOOD OR SLEEP ON AN UNCOMFORTABLE BED FOR A YEAR?

WOULD YOU RATHER...

... BE SUN OR MOON?

... TO WIN A MILLION DOLLARS AT ONCE OR WIN A LIFETIME SALARY OF $10,000 A MONTH?

WOULD YOU RATHER...

... TO HAVE ANGEL WINGS OR A MERMAID TAIL?

... TO WIN A MILLION DOLLARS AT ONCE OR WIN A LIFETIME SALARY OF $ 25,000 A YEAR?

WOULD YOU RATHER...

... TO HAVE ANGEL WINGS OR A MERMAID TAIL?

... NEVER LISTEN TO MUSIC OR NEVER HAVE PETS?

WOULD YOU RATHER...

... BE FAT AND HAVE A BEAUTIFUL FACE OR BE THIN AND HAVE AN UGLY FACE?

... TO INVENT AN INVENTION OR WRITE A WORLD BESTSELLER?

WOULD YOU RATHER...

... NOT HAVE TEETH
OR
NOT HAVE A TONGUE?

... BE ABLE TO WRITE FASTER THAN ANYONE OR SPEAK FASTER?

WOULD YOU RATHER...

... TO BE A UNIVERSITY PROFESSOR OR A COMPANY OWNER?

... BE ABLE TO WRITE FASTER THAN ANYONE OR SPEAK FASTER?

WOULD YOU RATHER...

... VISIT CANDY-LAND OR DISNEYLAND?

... HAVE 5 FRIENDS AND 10 FOES OR 10 FRIENDS AND 20 FOES?

WOULD YOU RATHER...

... ALWAYS WIN EVERY GAME OR HAVE ACCESS TO ALL GAMES FOR FREE?

... GO TO SCHOOL AT HOGWARTS OR LIVE IN NARNIA?

WOULD YOU RATHER...

... TO EAT PIZZA WITHOUT SAUCE
OR FRIES WITH ICE CREAM?

... LIVE WITH PENGUINS OR LEMURS?

WOULD YOU RATHER...

... BE A SUPERHERO OR A MAGIC WIZARD?

...TO EAT THREE ONIONS OR 5 CLOVES OF GARLIC?

WOULD YOU RATHER...

... A WARM WINTER OR A COLD SUMMER?

... GO FISHING
OR GO HIKING?

WOULD YOU RATHER...

... HAVE YOUR OWN ROBOT
OR
A JETPACK?

...TO HAVE A LITTLE PIG OR A LITTLE DEER?

WOULD YOU RATHER...

...BE STUNG BY A BEE ONCE
OR
BE BITTEN BY A MOSQUITO
10 TIMES?

...MEET A PERSON WHO LOOKS THE SAME AS YOU OR MEET A PERSON WHO HAS THE SAME CHARACTER AS YOU?

WOULD YOU RATHER...

... BE ABLE TO TALK TO ALL ANIMALS IN THE WORLD EXCEPT YOUR PET
OR
BE ABLE TO TALK ONLY TO YOUR PET?

... LIVE WITHOUT ELECTRICITY OR WITHOUT INDOOR PLUMBING?

WOULD YOU RATHER...

... HAVE A ROBOT OR A HELPER MONKEY?

... GO FOR A RIDE ON A SLEIGH WITH SANTA OR TAKE A BOAT TRIP WITH YOUR IDOL?

WOULD YOU RATHER...

...TO BE A SUPERSTAR OR A SUPERHERO SAVING PEOPLE?

... LOSE YOUR SENSE OF SMELL OR SENSE?

WOULD YOU RATHER...

...TO BE ABLE TO KNOW YOUR ANCESTORS OR
YOUR DESCENDANTS
WHO WILL LIVE IN 200 YEARS?

9 798565 462869